Original title:
The Greenhouse Poet

Copyright © 2025 Creative Arts Management OÜ
All rights reserved.

Author: Dexter Sullivan
ISBN HARDBACK: 978-1-80581-929-5
ISBN PAPERBACK: 978-1-80581-456-6
ISBN EBOOK: 978-1-80581-929-5

Verdure and Verse

In a pot of herbs, a poet grew,
With basil rhymes and sage that flew.
Each leaf a word, each stem a line,
In pesto dreams, the verse did shine.

Tomatoes giggled, cucumbers pranced,
While peppers plotted, they all danced.
In sunshine's glow, they played their part,
Crafting sonnets straight from the heart.

The Poetry of Rooted Souls

A radish claimed a sonnet's worth,
With roots entwined beneath the earth.
The carrots spoke in orange tones,
While lettuce whispered leafy moans.

A broccoli held a poetry slam,
While peas in pods sang, 'Oh, yes we am!'
They laughed at weeds that tried to tease,
But no one messes with these green knees!

Hushed Growth

In silence grows the garden's muse,
While crickets hum their nightly blues.
A creeping vine with secrets told,
In whispers soft, both funny and bold.

The flowers giggle, petals spin,
They'll flower up a quirky grin.
With jokes about the snails that crawl,
They make the quietest of all!

Vines of Imagination

A vine of dreams climbed high and free,
With thoughts that danced like bumblebees.
It wrapped around the thoughts of fun,
As sunlight chuckled, day begun.

Each tendril tickled, bursting smiles,
Creating joy that stretched for miles.
A tangle of ideas, wild and sweet,
With laughter growing from root to feet.

Sonnet of the Soil

In dirt, we plant our dreams so grand,
With worms as our loyal, squirming band.
I joke with weeds about their style,
They think they're chic? Oh, what a pile!

Sunshine giggles, clouds play hide,
While roots do waltzes deep inside.
The trowel's dance is quite a sight,
As we all laugh from morn 'til night.

Petals in the Prose

A daisy dressed in silly hues,
Tells tales of pollen and morning dews.
The roses pout with fragrant flair,
While tulips giggle – who has time to care?

Buds gossip low about the bees,
While butterflies float like they own the leaves.
In this garden of rhymes and cheer,
Nature's circus draws us near!

Nurtured by Nature's Hands

With watering can, I wield my might,
Planting seeds in hopes of height.
The radishes laugh and joke at me,
Saying, "We'll be roots, just wait and see!"

Squash shows off its glorious size,
While carrots plot in clever disguise.
I swear I heard a sprout yell, "Hey!"
As I stomp past on my garden way.

Lush Lines and Leafy Dreams

In leafy realms, the laughter flows,
Where every plant knows how humor grows.
Cucumber beats playing peekaboo,
While vines tangle up to craft the view.

Oh, what a sight, this green parade,
With broccoli jokes that never fade.
Laughter blooms in every seam,
As nature dances, wild and free.

Nature's Lyric Haven

In a garden of silly weeds,
The flowers learn to dance with ease.
A tulip told a joke so bright,
The daisies laughed till it was night.

A caterpillar wrote a play,
With snails as stars, they stole the day.
The bumblebees composed a tune,
While crickets crooned beneath the moon.

Petals of Reflection

A rose reflected on its face,
Said, "Mirror, mirror, I need space!"
The overlords of blooms agree,
It's hard to bloom and still be free.

The orchids, in their flashy clothes,
Gossip, and they strike a pose.
While sunflowers sunbathe all day,
In shades, they cheer, "Hip, hip, hooray!"

Beneath the Glass Ceiling

Inside a house of glass and light,
The plants have meetings late at night.
They plot their rise to leafy fame,
While laughing at their human frame.

Lettuce proposed to grow quite tall,
Said, "Let's outshine them, one and all!"
But the cactus raised a prickly hand,
"We need more room to help us stand!"

Fables in Filtration

The fountain told a tale so grand,
Of fish that danced upon dry land.
The lilies chuckled, "What a sight!"
A tale of absurdity and delight.

The frogs played cards, the bugs just laughed,
As water droplets made a draft.
In puddles bright, they slipped and slid,
Such antics from a splashy kid!

Words Entwined with Ferns

In a pot of puns, the ferns do sway,
Pretending to know what the buds will say.
Spouting rhymes like leaves in a breeze,
While cheeky roots wiggle with glee.

Cacti join in with a prickly grin,
Chiming in like they've got a spin.
Budding blooms giggle at their green wit,
As soil whispers jokes, never to quit.

Growth in Transience

A sprout once claimed it could dance on air,
But slipped on the dew; oh, what a scare!
Petals giggled, their colors ablaze,
As bees buzzed in mock, enjoying the craze.

Time ticked by with its own silly tune,
As weeds plotted mischief 'neath the bright moon.
Moss stitched together a quilt of green,
While worms wrote sonnets, a sight to be seen.

Verses of Vitality

The daisies debated, who's the best rhyme?
With petals aflutter, they ran out of time.
A tulip yelled, 'I bloom with a flair!'
While daisies just giggled, 'We don't have a care!'

In moments of giggles, the lilacs would chime,
Their verses of lavender creating sweet thyme.
But amidst all the chatter, a sunflower stood,
Spouting puns about sunshine, as all flowers should.

A Canopy of Creativity

Under green arches, the squirrels convene,
Their acorn confabs a comical scene.
A raccoon with glasses recites from a tome,
While roots pipe in with a rhythm of home.

With giggles of ferns and laughter from leaves,
They craft snacks of wisdom, no one believes.
As the sun sets low on this verdant display,
Their poetry dances, come join the bouquet!

Synchronicity of Seasons

Spring sings a tune of bright blooms,
While winter sneers with frosty glooms.
Summer dances with carefree flair,
Autumn mutters, "I'm almost there!"

Plants gossip, as they soak the light,
"Did you hear? The weather's a fright!"
They twist and twirl, quite the display,
As seasons joke and play all day.

The Canvas Under Glass

In a room with walls all clear,
Painted leaves dance, oh so near.
Colors burst like giggles free,
Canvas of life, who needs a tree?

A sunflower dons a silly hat,
While vines tangle like a playful cat.
Brushes dip in soil, not paint,
Art's no muse, just dirt's quaint!

Enchanted Greenery

Cacti wear sombreros, quite unique,
While ferns hold secrets we all seek.
Magic rules this little place,
Where plants giggle with silly grace.

Lettuce whispers, "Let's have a ball!"
Tomatoes reply, "We're having a ball!"
In this realm of leafy cheer,
Every twig has a wild frontier.

Stems of Significance

With stems so straight they strike a pose,
They pretend to be in fashion shows.
Daisies twirl in colorful styles,
Rooted deep, but making them smiles.

Wise old trees chuckle with pride,
"We were here before you, just look outside!"
Yet here they are, all dressed for fun,
In this botanical race, all are number one.

The Soul of a Leaf

A leaf whispered secrets in the breeze,
Telling tales of fluttering with ease.
It dreamed of being a kite someday,
But worried about winds that might sway.

In the sun, it tried a funny dance,
Twisting and twirling, taking a chance.
The bugs laughed hard, they couldn't agree,
'A leaf with moves? Now that's a spree!'

Reflections in the Roots

Beneath the soil, a party goes on,
Worms trade gossip from dusk till dawn.
Roots gossip about the flowers above,
"Hey, can we swap some sunshine and love?"

One root grumbled, 'I need some more space!'
"Don't get too comfy, you're hogging my place!"
The mushrooms giggled, exchanging their looks,
"Eavesdrop on roots, that's how you write books."

Sowing Seeds of Expression

I threw some seeds in a jiggly jig,
Hoping they'd blossom to do a big gig.
The daisies danced, the sunflowers swayed,
But the tomatoes just stood there, dismayed.

"Why can't we jam?" cried a sprightly sprout,
"Because," said a daisy, "you're too round and stout!"
But in that garden, laughter took flight,
Sowing joy beneath the starlit night.

Garden of Language

In a garden filled with giggles and glee,
Every plant spoke a word or three.
The lavender hummed a soothing tone,
While the snapdragons laughed with a groan.

"Let's form a band!" said the wise old tree,
"I'll play the trunk, and you'll sing with me!"
So they harmonized through sun and rain,
The garden burst forth with laughter again.

Nature's Muse

In the garden where weeds dance,
A snail takes on a silly stance.
The daisies giggle, quite a bit,
As ants debate, but none commit.

A frog leaps high with grand delight,
Chasing flies that dart in flight.
The daisies whisper, 'Catch that one!'
But oh, poor frog, he came undone!

The sun peeks out to join the fun,
Painting petals, everyone!
A bumblebee hums a tune so sweet,
While butterflies perform on tiny feet.

The time goes by in bursts of cheer,
For nature's jesters can appear.
In laughter blooms, we find our way,
Where every goof makes bright the day.

Canopy of Contemplation

Beneath the leaves, the squirrels chatter,
As acorns plummet—what's the matter?
They wiggle tails with such bravado,
While below, grass grows a bravado!

The clouds above play hide and seek,
Casting shadows, oh-so-weak.
A chipmunk rolls a nut with glee,
Then trips and lands by a peony!

The trees sway gently, side to side,
As owls make comments, quite snide.
With every breeze, a giggle flows,
Nature's comedy, who really knows?

In this green realm, joy's the decree,
Where every creature's wild and free.
So grab your hat, let's take our cue,
Life's a funny play—who knew?

Shadows of Serendipity

A hedgehog sings a tune off-key,
While butterflies roll, quite carefree.
The mushrooms bob their tiny heads,
In rhythm with the mossy beds.

Crickets tap dance on the grass,
As squirrels scuttle—what a sass!
The shadows stretch, do silly tricks,
As sunlight draws a bunch of flicks.

A wobbly beetle takes the stage,
As flowers fuel his tiny rage.
Each petal sways like it's on cue,
Nature's theater, who needs a zoo?

In patches where the laughter grows,
The air sings sweet, everyone knows.
So join the fun, don't let it stop,
In this comedic green backdrop!

Dwelling in Blooms

In blooms so bright, the bumblebees,
Forget their buzz, just laugh with ease.
The flowers share their juiciest jokes,
While daisies poke fun at the oaks.

A rose wears thorns like royal crowns,
While tulips twirl in silly gowns.
With each new bud, a prank's unfurled,
It's a whimsical flower world.

The violets giggle, taking bets,
On how much rain will raise the debts.
A playful breeze sweeps in so sly,
Tossing petals into the sky!

Thus nature laughs, in colors bold,
With every bloom, a tale is told.
So revel here, in this garden scene,
Where life is bright, and laughter's keen.

A Symphony of Seed and Syllable

In a garden where whispers grow,
Seeds wiggle, dancing in a row.
Beans wear hats, peas sport a tie,
Tomatoes giggle, oh my, oh my!

Sunflowers hum in a jolly tune,
Carrots march, they'll be out soon.
With every sprout, laughter flares,
Nature's chorus, joy declares!

A potato croons from its cozy bed,
Basil twirls 'round, dreams in its head.
Radishes trade their garden woes,
While lettuce laughs as the breezy blows.

A symphony where dirt's the stage,
Comedians sprout at every age.
With roots in puns and leaves of jest,
In this bright patch, we're all blessed!

Gazing through Glassy Frames

Peering through panes, a world so fair,
Lettuce winks in its verdant chair.
Cacti wear shades, oh what a sight,
Moss doing cartwheels, pure delight!

The peas recite poetry, oh so sweet,
As carrots tango with nimble feet.
Tomatoes gossip beneath the sun,
A drama unfolds, who'll be the one?

Sage suggests a party, bright and bold,
While thyme retells tales from days of old.
With every glance through glass so clear,
A riot of fun, we all cheer!

The orchids chuckle at their new neighbors,
Basil's humor, a hit with the labors.
In this glass realm where color beams,
Life's a show bursting at the seams!

Ode to the Hummingbird's Flight

Oh tiny wonder, quick and spry,
Darting like a wink in the sky.
Sipping nectar with loved delight,
A blur of colors, pure and bright.

You flit and flutter, a feathered tease,
Tickling blossoms, dancing with ease.
Your wings hum tunes that make us grin,
Every visit, a giggle wins.

You sip your drink, not a drop is missed,
In the busy buzz, you can't resist.
Onlookers laugh as you steal the show,
A mini acrobat, putting on a flow!

In gardens lush, you're the star of the day,
To every bloom, you've got much to say.
With every flight, a laugh in the air,
A tribute to joy, beyond compare!

Melodies Among the Moss

Amidst the green where shadows play,
Moss sings softly, hip hip hooray!
Mushrooms sway in their own slow dance,
A fungal fiesta, a rare romance.

Leaves gossip softly, secrets shared,
An audience gathered, all unprepared.
Nuts toss jokes from their cozy heights,
While the willow whispers to the nights.

Frogs croak choruses, ribbits abound,
In this green realm, laughter's profound.
Each moment fragrant, each giggle dear,
Nature's humor, serenely clear.

So let us join this merry crew,
With laughter ringing, pure and true.
Among the moss, beneath the trees,
Life's a song sung with ease!

Tending a Garden of Thoughts

In the plot where ideas sprout,
I plant my dreams, there is no doubt.
Watering them with silly schemes,
They bloom like flowers, bursting beams.

Weeds of worry I swiftly pluck,
Giggles grow, oh what good luck!
Roses blush with laughter bright,
Each petal sings, a pure delight.

Butterflies in silly hats,
Dancing 'round with chatty cats.
Sunshine tickles, shadows play,
In this garden, joy's the way.

So come along, don't be shy,
Join the fun, it's worth a try.
With every thought, a seed is sown,
In this crazy place, we've grown.

Vibrant Verses of Nature

In the meadow where laughter flows,
Witty daisies strike comedic poses.
Tulips don their brightest glows,
While squirrels debate, who really knows?

Nature's stage, a funny play,
Trees gossip in a breezy sway.
The sun grins wide, the clouds tease back,
In this theatre, joy's the knack.

The brook bubbles, tickling stones,
As frogs croak jokes in funny tones.
A cricket's chirp is quite the hit,
Nature's rhythm, a comedic skit.

So join the jest, don't miss the show,
Laughter's seeds are free to sow.
In vibrant shades of playful cheer,
This garden's humor draws us near.

Echoing Green

In the fields where chuckles cling,
The wind whistles a happy fling.
Grasshoppers host a joyful dance,
While daisies laugh at life's sweet chance.

With every echo, a joke takes flight,
Clouds giggle softly, what a sight!
A parrot sings in clashing tunes,
As sunbeams wink 'neath playful moons.

The brook's a stand-up, full of jokes,
As trees roll eyes and share their pokes.
Nature's band plays tunes so free,
In this world, we all agree.

So let's all laugh in this grand scene,
Where humor reigns, and life feels keen.
In echoes bright, let joy abound,
In every corner, laughter's found.

Hues of Harmony

In a garden where jokes bloom,
The daisies giggle, dispelling gloom.
A sunflower wears a bow tie wide,
While carrots dance with joyful pride.

Bumblebees buzz their silly songs,
As tomatoes laugh where they belong.
The peas play tag, they've lost their way,
Chasing shadows 'til the close of day.

The lettuce tells tales so absurd,
That even the radishes are disturbed.
With puns and riddles in every row,
This patch of fun has a vibrant glow.

So if you're down, just take a stroll,
Through this madcap, blooming knoll.
Where nature's laughter fills the air,
And every plant has a joke to share.

Eden's Embrace

In Eden's realm, the fruits conspire,
To form a band, a veggie choir.
They sing of seeds and sun's delight,
While avocado dons shades so bright.

Cucumbers roll in endless jest,
While peppers declare, "We're the best!"
A cheeky grape swings from a vine,
Sipping on dew, feeling divine.

The carrots chuckle at their length,
Flexing roots, showing off their strength.
Radishes paint their leaves with flair,
For every creature stops to stare.

So come and visit this playful land,
Where nature's laughter is always grand.
In the warm embrace of leafy grace,
You'll find a smile on every face.

Metaphorical Mulch

In the mulch where puns dig deep,
Worms wriggle while secrets keep.
A squash claims it's the funniest seed,
Spreading humor like a wild weed.

Underneath a leafy hat,
A snail raps about where he sat.
"I'm not slow, just taking my time,
Life's a journey, thought it could rhyme!"

Bees gossip while buzzing along,
Their sweet buzz turns into a song.
The daisies roll their eyes, it's true,
Some blooms are best with laughter too.

In this patch, there's joy abound,
With every plant, a smile found.
So spread the mulch, let humor reign,
In this garden where fun's never plain.

Tapestry of Trails

Wandering through a vibrant maze,
Every leaf has stories to raise.
A berry bursts with tart delight,
Making the baker grin with fright.

The trails are filled with jokey vines,
Where thyme and sage share silly lines.
"Lettuce dance!" the broccoli shouts,
While mushrooms prance, best friends, no doubts.

Nature's canvas, painted bright,
The colors hum in pure delight.
Even weeds wear a crown of cheer,
In this quirky garden, laughter's near.

So stroll the paths of laughter's grace,
Where every turn brings a smiling face.
In this whimsical, leafy terrain,
You'll find that joy can grow again.

Prayers Among the Petals

In the garden, whispers grow,
Petals dance, putting on a show.
Bumblebees with tiny hats,
Sipping nectar, they're the chitchat rats.

Worms recite their morning vows,
To the lettuce, they say, "You're ours!"
Marigolds giggle, faint and bright,
As the daisies join in the delight.

When snails roll by, that's quite a sight,
Synchronized like a slow dance fight.
Sunflowers laugh, they're in the mood,
For a wacky plant-based food feud.

And amid this floral jubilee,
Caterpillars brag, "Just wait for me!"
They'll flutter soon, with grace and glee,
A garden gala, oh, let's all see!

Sunbeam Serenade for the Heart

Sunlight tickles all the leaves,
Each beam a jester, nature weaves.
Flowers giggle in a line,
Telling shadows, "Not this time!"

The thorns whisper tales of care,
While daisies flaunt their golden hair.
Butterflies flutter, what a parade,
With jokes and jests, they're unafraid!

A breeze whooshes, "Catch me if you can!"
Wiggly vines play tag, oh what a plan!
Bees buzzing like a playful choir,
In the sun's embrace, they never tire.

This garden's like a carnival spree,
With laughter high as the tallest tree.
So let the rays paint the hearts so bright,
In this sunshine, everything feels right!

The Stitching of Soft Sunlight

Sunlight stitches through the gloom,
Creating joy, dispelling doom.
A tailor bee buzzes near,
With tiny thread, he brings a cheer.

Petunias wear polka-dot gowns,
Dancing around without any frowns.
Fungi in boots do a silly dance,
Inviting all to join their prance.

Garden gnomes tell tall tales,
Of mushroom ships and berry trails.
With every laugh, a sprout takes flight,
In this patch, everything's light!

Hang your troubles on a vine,
And laugh with us, we promise it's fine!
Let the petals tickle your soul,
In this soft sunlight, feel the whole!

Vessel of Verdant Inspirations

In a pot, the herbs debate,
Who's the fanciest on the plate.
Basil twirls in a fragrant dress,
While parsley claims, "I'm the best!"

A tomato sings in juicy tones,
Reminding everyone of his bones.
"I'll make you a salad, just you wait!"
The lettuce sighs, "Don't tempt fate."

Overhead, a squirrel is plotting,
Stealing acorns, very knotty and dotting.
While in the corner, a cabbage grins,
Challenging all to see who wins!

With laughter echoing through the green,
Every sprout knows it's quite a scene.
So plant your dreams in this garden wide,
Where humor blooms, and joy won't hide!

Sanctuary of Leaves

In a world where ferns wear hats,
And daisies gossip about the cats,
The bench is full of worms that chat,
While squirrels steal the poet's spat.

Sunlight dances on a vine,
Where lettuce thinks it's quite divine,
The carrots laugh, 'We're roots, not wine!'
A cabbage claims, 'I'm truly fine!'

Chickens here with tales so bold,
Share secrets of the plants of old,
Each seed a story to be told,
In this green space, laughter unfold.

With pots as hats and soil as shoes,
The daisies tease the poets' muse,
In this garden, there's no excuse,
For all the joy that we can use!

Echoes in the Canopy

In the trees, there's much to see,
Where squirrels swing with such esprit,
A parrot's name? Oh, what could it be?
'Polly Wanna, just fancy me!'

The branches rustle with delight,
As ladybugs take off in flight,
While mushrooms dance into the night,
And crickets strum a tune so bright.

Birds exchange a funny wink,
While spiders weave a yarn to think,
One plant claims, 'I'm on the brink!'
Of winning all the thoughts we ink!

Giggles echo through the leaves,
As laughter spills like summer eves,
In this place, the heart believes,
Where every word a humor weaves.

Cultivating Words

With trowels in our hands, we dig,
To plant a thought, both small and big,
Tomatoes share a juicy gig,
While peppers dance a salsa jig.

Each word a seed, we gently sow,
In soil where silly stories grow,
A rhyme here, and there, a flow,
As veggies trade their tales, you know.

A pumpkin tells of bumpy dreams,
And broccoli plots in veggie themes,
Zucchini giggles, nothing seems,
As funny folktales burst at seams!

In the garden, laughter's king,
Where nothing dull can dare to cling,
Every line we plant takes wing,
And joy's the harvest that we bring!

Secret Garden Soliloquies

Behind the gate, the flowers scheme,
With petals bright, they laugh and beam,
A lilac's whiff, a cheerful dream,
While thyme plays tricks on every theme.

The daisies plot their daily chat,
With garden gnomes who tip their hat,
While bees instruct the plants on that,
To write a tale, jesters in spat.

In hedges thick, the secrets swirl,
As ivy tends to twist and twirl,
A daffodil gives out a twirl,
To write a poem with a whirl!

Here's where the blooms all take the stage,
With petals open, they engage,
Each line a laugh, a funny page,
In this garden, we set the gauge.

Tangled Words in Trowel and Earth

In the garden where weeds dance,
I trowel words with a glance.
My plants giggle, quite absurd,
While I trip over my own word.

A flower whispers, 'Water me!'
I say, 'What? Just let it be!'
The sun rolls its golden eyes,
As I question my own wise ties.

But roots are deep, hopes remain,
Even when I drop my brain.
The daisies chuckle, ooh so sly,
As I plant seeds and sing goodbye.

Yet in this soil, laughter grows,
From tangled words the fun just flows.
With every leaf that sways and spins,
I find joy where the giggle wins.

Blossoming Thoughts in Bloom

Blossoms burst in colorful cheer,
While my thoughts wander, it's clear.
I forgot where I stashed the fork,
In this chaos, I'm a dork.

Petals fall like spoken jokes,
I'm laughing hard, just like the folks.
The tulips told me, 'Get a grip!'
But all I found was a gardening slip.

With every sprout, my mind takes flight,
We giggle as petals catch the light.
Thoughts blossom, but they often stray,
In this garden, it's a funny ballet.

I chase my mind among the green,
Where sunlight dances, bright and keen.
Every thought's a blossom thrown,
In a world where laughter's grown.

Harvesting Hope in Hues

With buckets wide, I chase the fruits,
My hope is tangled in silly roots.
I pluck a dream, it slips away,
Laughter mingles with the hay.

Carrots sprout like jokes in line,
I wonder where I left my rhyme.
Tomatoes blush from all the fun,
While I juggle them, my day's begun.

The corn stands tall, it seems to grin,
As I tumble, giggling in the spin.
I harvest bright from morning dew,
Each moment brings a funny view.

So here's to greens and vibrant hues,
In this patch where hope renews.
Each silly moment, like a seed,
Grows a garden of laughter, indeed!

Lyrics of the Leafy Canopy

Under leafy roofs, I sit tight,
The tree sings songs, what pure delight.
Its branches sway to breezy tunes,
While I dance like a silly raccoon.

The squirrels debate about their feast,
I giggle softly, nature's beast.
'Pass the acorns!' one does shout,
As I prance about, full of clout.

Each leaf flips like pages in a book,
With every rustle, a joyous look.
The canopy hums a playful song,
Where laughter lingers, all day long.

In this leafy space, I'm at ease,
Where smiles flutter like autumn leaves.
With lyrics bright, I join the play,
Under trees, I kiss worries away.

The Eden Within

In a tiny space, plants all collide,
Potting soil giggles, a sweet little ride.
A cactus is grumpy, the ferns like to tease,
Together they flourish, oh what a breeze!

Sunshine spills laughter from each little leaf,
A radish remarks, 'I'm the king of this chief!'
The beans dance around in a whimsical ball,
While the herbs gossip low, standing proud and tall.

Mushrooms look shy with their hats on so snug,
And peas do a jig, feeling ever so smug.
The basil winks at the tomato so ripe,
In this home of green, there's never a gripe!

So come join the fun, in this leafy retreat,
Where giggles abound and joy feels complete.
In every sprout's story, there's humor well told,
In the Eden within, let your laughter unfold.

Conversations with Chlorophyll

Chlorophyll sat, sipping dew in a cup,
'Why can't we just dance? Let's all light up!'
The marigolds joke, 'We outshine the sun,'
While daisies simp, 'Who's the prettiest one?'

Potted pals share their pots and their dreams,
While succulents grumble, 'We make best teams!'
Herbs barter secrets to smoothies they craft,
As carrots retort, 'We're rootin' for laughs!'

'I know a great song about turning to face,'
Said the sunflower, reaching for space.
Leaves join the chorus, and all of them sway,
In harmonized laughter, they brighten the day.

With every soft rustle, each branch has a tale,
Of sunshine and raindrops that tell of the scale.
So tune in, dear friend, to this verdant chat,
For wisdom and giggles all grow on the mat!

Ode to the Living Canvas

A canvas of green with colors so bright,
Each brushstroke of nature a whimsical sight.
The vines twist and twirl in a painterly glee,
While daisies add dots, as happy as can be.

The roses paint love, each petal a kiss,
'Hold my hand, dear stem, let's not go amiss!'
The daisies love whispers, the pansies love cheers,
In our garden of joy, there's laughter for years!

Amidst splashes of petals, the colors converge,
While sunflowers giggle, as their heads do emerge.
Canvas of laughter, in hues bold and true,
Creating a masterpiece with each morning dew.

So grab a paintbrush, join the delight,
In this living canvas, everything's bright.
For art grows and flows, and oh, what a treat,
Let the garden's giggles be your heartbeat!

Blossoms of Inspiration

Beneath the big sky, a wonderland grows,
Where blossoms of laughter and mischief bestow.
With petals like jokes, each bloom is a jest,
Sprouting bright smiles in their colorful vest.

The tulips chortle as the daisies talk back,
'You think you're so fresh, but I'm on the track!'
With stems all entwined in a whimsical race,
The garden's a stage, a plant-based showcase!

'Why do flowers blush?' asks the green bell pepper,
'When bees come to flirt, they just love the stepper!'
And laughter erupts from each leafy soul near,
Blooming inspiration, a jest without fear.

So take a wild stroll through this playful expanse,
Where blossoms are giggles and humor's the dance.
In this patch of delight, let your spirit be free,
For life's just a garden—come laugh here with me!

Poetic Petals

In the garden of rhymes, flowers do giggle,
Petals dance round, with a playful wiggle.
Bees buzz in tune, as verses take flight,
While snails race each other, oh what a sight!

Worms write their sonnets, on a moist page,
Telling tales of soil and a burrowing sage.
Sunshine spills laughter, on leaves all aglow,
As daisies put on their bright yellow show.

Laughter erupts from a tulip's bright cup,
Who knew blooms had jokes that could lift you up?
Gardens as stages, where plants steal the scene,
Petal-powered puns that are ripe and serene.

With every soft breeze comes a chuckle, a cheer,
Nature's own circus, where all can appear!
So join in the fun, let your worries take flight,
In this whimsical garden, where joy reigns delight.

Trellis of Thought

Climbing thoughts like vines, reaching for sky,
Twisting ideas, as they laugh and fly.
A trellis of wit, where the silly can grow,
With grape-like jokes that just won't let go.

Lattice of laughter, let your mind roam,
Each twist and turn feels just like home.
A squash makes a pun, with a giggle so bright,
While tomatoes roll by, just for a bite.

In this garden of minds, where ideas entwine,
Each flower of thought drinks up sunshine.
So pluck a good notion, let joy take its stand,
In this zany domain, lend a helping hand.

Raise up your quips on the sturdy old beams,
Snap at the jokes, like a plant in the streams.
With every new thought, let your spirits abound,
In the trellis of chuckles, true treasure is found.

Fragrance of Imagery

Whiffs of wild whimsy waft through the air,
Painted skies wink, as flowers do care.
A daisy dreams loud, in shades so profound,
While tulips tell tales without making a sound.

Inhale the absurd, let it tickle your nose,
As scents of imagination blossom and pose.
Each sprout is a story that beckons and glows,
Like popcorn and butter in a whimsical throes.

The parsley's a poet, as spicy as rhyme,
In the garden of humor, it's simply sublime.
Carrots dub themselves the orange-fingered, sly,
Painting worlds with colors that don't just comply.

So waft up a giggle, let humor take flight,
In this fragrant delight, everything feels right.
With each fragrant note that your senses perceive,
The imagery dances, and your heart will believe.

Leafy Lullabies

Leaves whisper softly, in the hush of the night,
Telling tales of laughter, 'neath the soft moonlight.
Frogs croak in tune, with crickets as choir,
Strumming up dreams on a leaf-covered lyre.

Branches sway gently, as if in delight,
To the rhythm of giggles in the stillness so bright.
A firefly's flicker adds sparkle and glee,
While owls hoot jokes, from a nearby tree.

Roots hold their secrets, as the soil will sigh,
As a leaf softly hums, letting worries fly high.
In this symphony, leafed with sweet cheer,
Nature sings lullabies, bringing joy near.

So drift on a breeze, where the funny resides,
Beneath dancing branches, where wonder abides.
Here bedtime stories are woven with light,
In leafy embraces, all troubles take flight.

Whispers of Verdant Sanctuary

In a garden where veggies talk,
Tomatoes tell tales, and corns just gawk.
Peppers dance in a raunchy jig,
While broccoli flexes, feeling big.

A lettuce leaf with a gossip game,
Whispers secrets of the plants to fame.
The herbs chuckle, their laughter tall,
As daisies gossip at the foot of the wall.

Oh, the radishes roll in mirthful strife,
'Who needs the sun when we've got life?'
Cucumbers giggle as they reach their prime,
Making punchlines ripe for garden rhyme.

Even the soil joins in the jest,
Planting humor where roots invest.
In this patch of loud and leafy lore,
Laughter blossoms forevermore.

Blooms Beneath Glass

Under glass, the flowers grin wide,
They poke their heads, full of pride.
A cactus cracks jokes, sharp and dry,
While daisies roll eyes, oh me, oh my!

The orchids declare themselves royalty,
With crowns of petals for all to see.
"Don't forget the weeds," a tulip quips,
"Even thorns can have the best of flips!"

Sunflowers stand tall, striking a pose,
As bees swarm in, singing their prose.
The leaves wave hands to the gardening crew,
"Join the fun; we have work to do!"

Every bloom brings a twist of delight,
In the sunlit refuge, home to the bite.
So let the laughter and blooms interlace,
Under the glass, in this bright place!

Echoes in the Sunlit Haven

In a sunlit spot where cheer runs free,
The daisies are twirling, just look and see!
A gnome tells jokes about his lost hat,
While the violets giggle, 'What's up with that?'

The ferns flip fables in leafy tones,
With merry sounds that tickle the bones.
Carrots chuckle, buried deep in the ground,
They love a good pun that's humor-bound!

Every seedling sprouts netted with joy,
"Plant a good laugh," says a sprightly soy.
The sunshine bathed plants all join the fray,
In this lively show, they dance and play.

With echoes of laughter, the day flies by,
In this playful haven 'neath the wide blue sky.
A medley of giggles, blooms all around,
In sunlit whispers, a joy profound!

Reflections of Leafy Verses

In a patch where squirrels take high tea,
Spinach sways, feeling sprightly and free.
Mint sips laughter, a refreshing brew,
While beans crack jokes, oh what a crew!

Petunias quick with a comical stare,
Dissecting clouds with botanical care.
In this verse of leaves, we enchant the day,
Where rhymes are seeded in a humorous way.

From fig leaves to sprouts that leap with glee,
Every plant plays a part in this jubilee.
The sun shines bright on this leafy spree,
As laughter greets roots with wild esprit.

So here's to the mischief in nature's design,
Where humor grows thick on the tendril line.
In leafy verses, happiness we find—
Nature's own jesters, so clever and kind.

Blooms of Awareness

In a garden of thoughts, I first misread,
A dandelion laughed, 'You're lost in your head!'
With petals like pages, they turned with glee,
'This book of blooms is the life of me.'

The tulips debated who'd wear the best robes,
While roses struck poses, inflating their probes.
But bees in the sun danced a tango of love,
While snails slowly cheered them from below, above.

A gopher, quite cheeky, dug up a tale,
Of carrot conspiracies, intriguing and frail.
He swore on a glyph, a secret he'd found,
Of how veggies get worried when pests are around.

So here's to the blooms, with laughter so bright,
In this wacky green world, we'll thrive with delight.

Whispered Wisps of Green

In a forest of whispers, leaves giggled in jest,
Squirrels swapped secrets, each claimed to be best.
A fern, rather sassy, boasted of style,
While ferns on the side rolled their eyes with a smile.

Bumblebees buzzed with a rhythm divine,
They formed a conga line, a dance so fine.
The flowers were shocked, couldn't find their own feet,
As petals all tumbled, caught up in the beat.

The mushrooms all chuckled, with caps worn so proud,
'This party's inclusive, let's shout it out loud!'
A wise old oak chuckled, 'I'm here for the shade,'
While vines crept around, like they just made the grade.

So sway with the breeze, let laughter take flight,
In this merry green realm, everything feels right!

Mosaic of Moss

On rocky old stones, in patches we find,
A mosaic of moss, nature's artsy kind.
Each tuft tells a story, of dew drops and sun,
The green artists giggling, they're oh so much fun!

A snail in a tutu slides by with some flair,
He twirled on the moss while the frogs stopped to stare.
They croaked in approval, a concert of cheer,
As squirrels drummed up rhythms, the tempo was clear.

The chic little lichen, in shades of the best,
Wore glasses and hats, oh what quite the zest.
Sprout parties exploded in patches of glee,
While ants with their snacks gathered, happy as can be.

A waltz on the stones, as twilight set in,
The moss kept on laughing, a soft, joyous grin.

Nature's Narrative

In the pages of nature, stories unfold,
With critters as characters, whimsical, bold.
A firefly author penned tales in the night,
While crickets composed with the stars shining bright.

The plot twists and turns through the whispering trees,
With antics of hedgehogs and giggles from bees.
The wise owl narrates with a deep, chirpy tone,
His audience chuckles, never alone.

A deer in a sweater got stuck in some brambles,
She chuckled aloud, 'What a comedy gambles!'
With a splash and a dash, froggies leaped with delight,
Creating a ruckus, oh what a wild sight!

As the sun dipped low, and shadows came in,
Nature's grand book closed, with laughter akin.
For every sweet moment, a giggle or two,
In the open air theater, where joy bloomed anew.

Nature's Dialogue

In the garden, plants do chatter,
A rose jokes, 'I'm no sad flatter!'
The daisies giggle, swaying light,
While the sun beams, oh what a sight!

The carrots whisper, 'We dig so deep,'
Tomatoes blush while secrets they keep.
A squirrel rolls by with a cheeky grin,
And claps the beans for their shiny skin.

The herbs gossip under the moon's delight,
Sage says, 'Gossip's quite a tasty bite!'
They dance in the breeze, a comedic show,
Nature's own circus, with a splash of wow!

Then comes the rain, an unruly guest,
Making puddles where the frogs can jest.
Laughter echoes through the colorful blooms,
As joy brews softly in nature's rooms.

Leaves of Lyrical Light

Leaves swirl down like playful notes,
Tickling the grass, in joy it floats.
The wind teases with a whiff of grass,
And whispers secrets as the squirrels pass.

This tree's a comedian, branches all bent,
With roots that giggle, oh, what a blend!
A leaf shakes hands with a curious bee,
Says, 'Join our dance, come jig with me!'

The sunlight chuckles, flickering bright,
While shadows chuckle, joining the fight.
Into the air, their laughter soars,
A musical riot as nature explores!

So here in the woods, laughter is free,
As each little critter sings in glee.
With a tap of a root and a sway of a vine,
The stage is set—how perfectly divine!

Frame of Nature's Palette

In this canvas, brush strokes of green,
Sprouts joy and laughter, a vibrant scene.
With flowers that giggle, and trees that grace,
Nature paints smiles, no need for a trace.

Old gnarled branches wave, 'Hooray!'
While daisies nod, hip-hip-hooray!
Colors competing for the sun's warm kiss,
Each bloom promising a hug or a bliss.

The clouds join in, a fluffy brigade,
Casting funny shapes while the sun does cascade.
A painter's dream, a joyful sprawl,
Nature's palette always ready to enthrall!

With emerald greens blending with bright yellows,
Leaves rustle laughter, nature's own fellows.
Brushstrokes of whimsy everywhere found,
In this masterpiece, giggles abound.

The Breath of Botanicals

Plants puff laughter into the air,
Cacti grin widely, not a single care.
The ferns flutter soft, like whispers of cheer,
As daisies dance, spreading joy far and near.

With every gust, the petals all sway,
'Join us!' they sing, in their floral ballet.
Nature's own orchestra, a comical tune,
Balloons of breath, gently float 'neath the moon.

Roots tickle the soil, making it laugh,
While bushy blooms trade a funny craft.
A shrub suggests a picnic parade,
While the roses cheer, 'Don't be afraid!'

In this botanical plunge, fun's on display,
Giggles and chuckles are here to stay.
So come, take a breath, let nature's song flow,
In a world where the silliness surely will grow.

Breath of the Botanical Muse

In a garden so lush, the plants take a stand,
Giggling leaves, they all wave their hands.
A cactus told jokes, it caused quite a sting,
While the daisies just laughed at each silly fling.

Sunflowers dance with the breeze all around,
They twist and they twirl, such joy to be found.
A fern told a secret, then tickled a sprout,
'You've got quite the style, no doubt about that!'

The beans made a band, played tunes with delight,
Their rhythm was funky, the vibe was just right.
A carrot once said, 'let's sprout some good cheer,'
While the turnips held hands and sang loud and clear.

So here in this realm where the green dreams reside,
Laughter is blooming; oh, what a wild ride!
With humor and growth, the plants sing and sway,
In their world of green joy, they brighten the day.

Canvas of Color and Care

With pots full of color, the garden's a sight,
Each hue tells a story, it's pure delight.
A rose wore a hat, all decked out in style,
While the violets giggled, they stayed for a while.

The tulips were painting with laughter and glee,
Splashing bright colors as happy as can be.
A zucchini moonwalked, quite smooth on the ground,
While marigolds cheered, it was joy all around.

The lettuce threw parties, with crunchy fresh fun,
It invited the chives; they danced 'til they spun.
A jolly old gourd told a tale with a grin,
Of how every vegetable fits in the bin.

So here in this patch where the funny things bloom,
Each plant has its story, it brightens the room.
With laughter as paint, they create and they share,
A whimsical garden, a canvas laid bare.

Whispers of Verdant Dreams

In the hush of the garden, secrets unfold,
The leaves whisper softly, their tales to be told.
A radish named Red liked to play tricks,
While the bushes around shared their favorite picks.

The mint gave advice, with a sprightly brew,
"Stay fresh and delightfully green, it's true!"
The peas in their pods were up to some fun,
They rolled in the dirt, all just for a pun.

The morning glories laughed, as they twined up the fence,

Saying, "Life's like a vine, it's so much more intense!"
A petunia joked, "Why'd the flower get lost?
Because it followed its nose, and paid the cost!"

So here in this space, where joy blooms in seams,
The garden is filled with these whimsical memes.
With laughter and love, every bud learns to beam,
In a world that's alive with verdant dreams.

In Blooming Verses

In verses of blooms, the stories do flow,
Each petal a word, a twirling tableau.
A daffodil whispered a pun from the past,
While a rose had a riddle that tickled and cast.

The daisies agreed to throw a big bash,
They invited the weeds, with snacks made of trash!
A sunflower said, "Let's dance through the night,"
While the larkspur just gawked at this incredible sight.

A peony posed with flair and surprise,
"Blooming is fun when you're clever and wise!"
The violets chuckled, all blue and quite bold,
As the tales from the garden began to unfold.

In this vibrant place, humor's always in bloom,
Where laughter and joy suddenly fill up the room.
With verses alive and each flower a verse,
The garden sings out, in colorful verse.

Serenity in Succulents

In pots they sit, so proud and green,
Chubby leaves that rarely preen.
Whisper secrets, they don't fuss,
Just soak up sun without a rush.

A cactus tried to make a friend,
But poked too hard, it had to bend.
A succulent with attitude,
Claims it's a plant, not food or brood.

When watering day rolls around,
They shiver, fidget, then rebound.
A dance of joy, all crammed in rows,
Happiness blooms, everybody knows!

So here we are, in leafy cheer,
A garden circus, come draw near.
Let's laugh with plants, and share a grin,
In this wild world where greens begin.

Verdant Voices

A fern once sang a pop hit tune,
While ivy danced beneath the moon.
Potted pals, they form a band,
Strumming leaves, oh isn't it grand?

Kale tried out for a veggie role,
But sprouted legs, lost all control.
Spinach whispered jokes so sly,
Even broccoli learned to fly!

Amidst the dirt, secrets we share,
Unearthing laughter hangs in the air.
The soil chuckles with every sprout,
In this wild world, there's no doubt!

So let's put on a leafy play,
Where plant dreams bloom and laugh all day.
With nature's joy, we'll find our voice,
In greens and giggles, let's rejoice!

Syllables of Sunlight

A sunflower peeked with a big broad smile,
Claiming sunshine was worth the while.
With petals bright and stem so tall,
It winked at bees, who'd come to call.

Lilies whispered secrets of grace,
While daisies giggled, a sunny race.
They played tag with the passing breeze,
Clutching droplets like precious keys.

A tomato threw a salsa bash,
But forgot the chips—what a clash!
Yet radishes wore a funky hat,
Declaring, "Join us, where you're at!"

Every leaf sings with joy to provide,
A rhyme of nature that can't be denied.
In this garden, where humor grows,
Syllables dance like sprightly prose.

Blooming Introspection

A daffodil thought, "What's the plan?"
"Should I keep growing or learn to tan?"
With petals stretched in warm sunlight,
It pondered much, day turned to night.

A wise old oak gave thoughts so stout,
"Just be you, what's life without doubt?"
As daisies giggle in perfect rows,
They share their dreams of earthy prose.

Pansies sighed, "What a time to be!"
"Growing old just means we're free."
A sprout said, "Count your leaves, they say,
Each year's a ring, let's bloom and play!"

So let us flourish, dance, and twirl,
In this garden, let laughter unfurl.
With roots in joy and blooms in jest,
We celebrate life, give it our best.

Sowing Words in Fertile Ground

In a field of giggles, seeds are sown,
Messy verses sprout, occasionally blown.
Watered with laughter, sunshine's embrace,
Each line grows wild, setting a merry pace.

Worms wear top hats, dancing in rows,
Weeds tell jokes, as the soft wind blows.
Cabbages chuckle, peas leap in glee,
Planting puns, as happy as can be.

Sunflowers nod, with cheeky grins wide,
Tomatoes blushing, trying to hide.
In this garden, humor takes flight,
Sowing words, oh what a delight!

Chasing the clouds, they hop and they swing,
Each line a song, oh how they sing.
In fertile ground, where laughter is found,
Growing giggles, all around.

The Choreography of Growing Dreams

With a hat on sideways, I step to the beat,
Plants do the cha-cha, oh what a treat!
Dancing with daisies, jumping with joy,
Each step a pun, like a playful toy.

The carrots are twirling, in the morning light,
Radishes waltz, such a comical sight.
Choreographed chaos in rows oh so neat,
Growing dreams that wiggle and twist on their feet.

Lettuce does limbo, while beans do a jig,
Bouncing off rhymes, oh so big!
Caught in a spin, I can barely keep track,
As flowers pitch in for a playful quack.

Under the moon, with shadows that sway,
The garden's a stage where laughter will play.
Choreography blooms in whimsical streams,
In this dance of life, we harvest our dreams.

Twilight's Lullaby in Nature's Cradle

As the day yawns wide, with a wink and a sigh,
Fireflies shimmer, like stars in the sky.
Crickets compose a soft lullaby tune,
While the garden hums beneath the full moon.

Petunias whisper secrets, juicy and bright,
Bees in pajamas dream sweetly at night.
The vining tendrils stretch, searching for fun,
While dreaming of races, they dash 'til they're done.

A gentle breeze tickles, the leaves giggle back,
Sleepy buds cuddle, all in a stack.
Nature's own cradle rocks softly in dreams,
Where everything's funny, nothing's as it seems.

As twilight wraps all in its velvety fold,
Dreamers awake, with tales to be told.
In this hush of night, laughter's embraced,
In the cradle of nature, joys interlaced.

Resounding Among the Roots

Underneath the soil, laughter takes root,
Tickling the earth, in whimsical loot.
Giggling fungi, with jokes in their cap,
Rabbits are chuckling, cuddled in nap.

With the rain's soft chatter, the trees join in,
Their branches sway lightly, like a playful spin.
Whispers of rhymes, as the soil hums loud,
Echoing humor, drawing in a crowd.

Wiggly worms share tales, spinning and neat,
Down in the dirt, they organize a fleet.
Each root is a story, alive with delight,
Growing up laughter, throughout the night.

In this merry underground, joy intertwines,
Where the puns take hold and the wit brightly shines.
Resounding among roots, where fun is renowned,
In life's vibrant garden, great giggles abound.

www.ingramcontent.com/pod-product-compliance
Lightning Source LLC
Chambersburg PA
CBHW070322120526
44590CB00017B/2784